THE GENESIS BRIEF: THE SIN FACTOR

SYLVIA RICHARDSON

Copyright © 2015 by Sylvia Richardson
Los Angeles, California
All rights reserved
Printed and Bound in the United States of America

Published and Distributed by:
Professional Publishing House
1425 W. Manchester Ave. Ste B
Los Angeles, California 90047
323-750-3592
Email: professionalpublishinghouse@yahoo.com
www.Professionalpublishinghouse.com

Cover design: TWA Solutions
First Printing: January 2015
978-0-9891960-2-4
10987654321

No part of this book may be reproduced, stored in a retrieval system or transmitted in any form or by any means without the prior written permission of the publisher — except by a reviewer who may quote brief passages in a review to be printed in a newspaper, magazine or journal.

For inquiries contact the publisher.

DEDICATION

This book is dedicated to all who seek truth.

ABOUT THE AUTHOR

SYLVIA RICHARDSON, a native Californian, is a mother of one, Aaron Andrews, and has three wonderful grandchildren: Destiny, Lalani, and baby Aaron. Sylvia is a teacher of young children in Los Angeles. She also writes children's books, and is an inventor as well. Sylvia's goal in *The Genesis Brief* is to make the Bible-reading community take a deeper look into the Word of God in order to get a more profound understanding of the God of the Bible.

TABLE OF CONTENTS

Chapter One: If Heaven Were a Perfect Place, and It Is, How Did Sin Originate There? 9

Chapter Two: Were there People on Planet Earth Before Adam? And if so, Why? 19

Chapter Three: The Covenant and the Man 30

Chapter Four: Adam's Covenant Partner, the Help Meet 33

Chapter Five: The Children of the Covenant 60

Chapter Six: Sons of God 72

Overview of Brief Points 98

CHAPTER One

If Heaven Were a Perfect Place, and It Is, How Did Sin Originate There?

If heaven were a perfect place, and it was, and it is, as it will always be, then how did sin originate there? Yes, sin did originate in the third heaven, the heaven where God, his Son Jesus, and his holy angels live. Revelation 12:7 says, *And there was a war in heaven; Michael and his angels fought against the dragon; and the dragon fought and his angels.* Verse 8, *And prevailed not; neither was there place found any more in heaven.* Verse 9, *And the great dragon was cast out, that old serpent, called the Devil, and Satan, which deceiveth the whole world: he was cast out into the earth, and his angels were cast out with him.* So the scriptures are clear about where Satan came from, and this could also be the reason why the whole earth was water in the beginning when God began to create and call forth.

Genesis 1:1 states, *In the beginning, God created the heaven and the earth.* Verse 2, *And the earth was void; and darkness was upon the face of the deep. And the Spirit of God moved upon the face of the waters.* Water, as we know, purifies, so when God began to create and call forth in the earth, he first purified it with water and the washing of his Word (Ephesians 5:26). Although the verse is about Paul speaking to the husbands loving their wives, God's Word applies and is true here. When God spoke this world into creation, his Word sanctified it and set it aside for his covenant people to have a spirit-to-spirit relationship with his greatness. So great is God that he had a desire to share it with a covenant people, a people that had his heart, and his mind. So multifaceted, so vast, so wide, so deep, so rich, so loving is God that he could not keep him to himself.

But let's get back to the sin and the war that took place in heaven. Genesis 2:9 says, *And out of the ground made the*

Lord God to grow every tree that is pleasant to the sight, and good for food: and that the tree of life also was in the midst of the garden, and the tree of knowledge of good and evil. So the tree of life, as well as the tree of knowledge of good and evil, did not grow but was placed there by God himself.

Revelation 22:1-2 states that God shows John a pure river of water of life, as clear as crystal, proceeding out of the throne of God and of the Lamb. Verse 2 tells us that in the midst of the street of it, and on either side of the river, was THE TREE OF LIFE. Revelation 2:7 says that *to him that overcometh will I give to eat of the tree of life, which is in the midst of the paradise of God.* Therefore, if the tree of life is in the third heaven with God, where one day we will be able to eat of it, then this tree of life is the same tree of life that was in the Garden of Eden, and if the tree of life was in the Garden of Eden, it once was in heaven in his paradise before it was on earth. And if this same tree of life was in heaven, then the tree of knowledge of good and evil must have been in heaven as well at some time.

This tree of life was never touched or eaten by Adam or Eve, because they would have never sinned had they partook of it, because the tree of life brings not only life, but wisdom, righteousness, and wholesomeness. Proverbs 3:18 informs us that *she is a tree of life to them that lay hold upon her.* Proverbs 11:30 tells us, *The fruit of the righteous is a tree of life.* Proverbs 12:28 states, *In the way of righteousness is life: and in the pathway thereof is no death.* Proverbs 15:4 expresses, *A wholesome tongue is a tree of life.* Not that Adam and Eve didn't already possess these attributes, but had they eaten of the tree of life, they (Eve) would have known this wisdom and would not have been able to be tricked by the devil.

The tree of life as well as the tree of the knowledge of good and evil, I believe, originated in heaven. Did God create evil angels? The short answer is *absolutely not!!* Ezekiel 28:15 states, *Thou was perfect in thy ways from the day thou was created, till iniquity was found in thee.* So when did this once beautiful angel called Lucifer come to be evil? Ezekiel 28:13-15 speaks of his beauty and perfection.

The Genesis Brief: The Sin Factor

Let's go back to the trees that I believe were once in heaven—the tree of life and the tree of the knowledge of good and evil (which, by the way, this Garden of Eden where God placed Adam was a prototype of God's garden which is in heaven. See Ezekiel 28:13, Revelation 21:19-21, and Revelation 22:1-2).

It has been said that angels don't have wills; they (angels) just go about doing and being to God much like robots. But not only do angels have a will, they also have personalities, and jobs, and ranks to fit these personalities they have. What they don't have are free wills, and what they don't have are bodies, and what they can not do is die, so they cannot be redeemed. With this in mind, I believe Lucifer, while yet of the heavenly host, out of curiosity, not evilness, took of this tree of the knowledge of good and evil while it was still in heaven, and became evil incarnate! Lucifer then began to know and become all manner of evil out of a curious will that first started in heaven with this tree of the knowledge of good and evil.

God has no blood covenant with angels, for angels have no flesh and blood, so this tree of the knowledge of good and evil was not forbidden in heaven as it was forbidden with God's covenant people, Adam. Now, after Lucifer had taken of this tree and had become evil incarnate, "the evil one," a now-changed being from the once beautiful, with harmonious music built right into him declaring the glory of the Lord, he is now quite the opposite of beauty, love, truth, and life, itself, and has become "the fallen one." He is fallen from his original state. He is a spirit, and was kicked out of the physical place heaven, and never again was there found a place for him there (Revelation 12:8).

Jude 1:6 says, *And the angels which kept not their first estate, but left their own habitation, he hath reserved in everlasting chains under darkness unto judgment of that great day.* So, he was sent to this earth and was made a hell to live in, one day forever and ever. Isaiah 14:12 says, *How art thou fallen from heaven, O Lucifer, son of the morning! how art thou cut down to the ground to weaken the nations!* Verse 13 explains, *For thou hast said in thine heart, I will ascend into heaven, I will exalt my throne above the stars of God: I will sit also upon the mount of the congregation.* Verse 14 continues, *I will ascend above the heights of the clouds; I will be like the most high God.* Verse 15 states, *Yet thou shalt be brought down to hell.* These verses tell us that angels do have a will (I WILL!). Verse 12 lets us know that Lucifer has come from heaven, or fallen out of heaven, and verse 15 lets us know that hell is where he will ultimately end up.

Now after Lucifer had taken from this tree of knowledge of good and evil and had become evil incarnate, he then persuaded about a third part of the angelic host to do as he did and partake of this tree. They too became evil after being persuaded by Lucifer that this tree was the best thing to happen to them.

Now Lucifer, who was always a leader of the angelic host, is now the leader of sin and all things evil. He and his now imps whom he has beguiled, have become so prideful because of their sin. Lucifer has become even more prideful because of his rank and beauty. He decided he will lead a revolution, a revolt, a war, in order to dethrone the Most

High God. We can begin to see how sin can lie to you, make you believe you can do without God. Sin makes one to believe that they can be self-willed and not God-willed, or self-centered as opposed to God-centered. All righteous thought is now self-centered, self-willed, and becomes all about what I want. I will. I will. I will. It is just another way of saying *my will* and not *God's will* anymore. And so, Lucifer fell. Lucifer partook of the tree of knowledge of good and evil, persuaded a third of the angels to do the same, and a war ensued. They lost and got kicked out.

And now, if this is true of the fallen ones' account, then this is exactly what Lucifer did to Eve. But more about Eve later.

Lucifer's intended purpose was now turned into the opposite of what God had created him to be, and this is what the devil is trying to still do today to God's people to get them off their intended purpose, God's purpose, and get them into their will, their fallen will, and not God's will. Yes, the fallen one is still up to his old tactics. He is still the same defeated foe, with the same fallen, sinful ideas—to drag as many into hell with him as possible, the same way he persuaded a third of the angelic host to believe his lie, and dragged them out of heaven with him, right into hell so he wouldn't be alone in the fires of hell. No, he didn't want to be alone in hell, with his own lies, for he is the father of lies, since he became the evil one once he partook of the tree of knowledge of good and evil.

The only one able to handle this tree was the creator of this tree itself; that is, God, the Father of Life, for he is the Life of the tree of life, and the Handler of knowledge, both good and evil.

Let me stop here and ask everyone that has not yet chosen life to do so now. Stop allowing the devil to lie to you. Choose Life. Ask Jesus to come into your heart and remake you back into his image and his likeness, as it was intended to be before the lie, before the fall of Lucifer. He is the defeated one. Remember when the war ensued in heaven and he lost, he prevailed not (Revelation 12:7-8).

Don't be a loser like the devil. Ask Christ to come into your heart and make you a winner, to give you life . . . his life on this earth and in his heaven one day.

CHAPTER
Two

Were There People on Planet Earth Before Adam? And if so, Why?

*E*cclesiastes 3:1: *To everything there is a season, and a time to every purpose under the heaven.*

Genesis 1:26 tells us that after God created all the heavens and the earth, and the trees, all kinds of plant life, all manner of animals, both in and out of the ocean, he said, *And God said, let us make man in our image, after our likeness: and let THEM have dominion over the fish of the sea, and over the fowl of the air, and over the cattle, and over all the earth, and over every creeping thing that creepeth upon the earth.* In other words, over all that he created including the earth itself. Verse 27: *So God created man in his own image, in the image of God created he him; male and female created he them.* So here the Bible tells us that God created both a man and a woman at the same time, but made them different from the animal kingdom in that they were made in the image and likeness of God, and he gave them (man and woman) power over all. The God-given purpose is higher in man than in the animal kingdom.

Then God did and said to man the same as he did with the animal kingdom. He blessed them, or enabled them to do as he was about to command to them their purpose, which was . . . to be fruitful, and multiply, and to replenish the earth; to subdue it and to have dominion over all he had created (Genesis 1:28).

In Genesis 1:29, God goes on to tell this man and woman what they were to eat. Genesis 1:31 says, God saw that it (all he had created) was very good. Genesis, chapter 2, verse 1, states that *Thus the heavens and the earth were finished, and all the host of them.* Verse 2 tells us that on the seventh day God rested from all his work he had made. Now this "rest" that God did on the seventh day was a temporary stop. God stopped temporarily so what he commanded to be could be. For instance, God commanded that the waters bring forth abundantly, or to multiply. God called for the winged creatures to multiply, for all cattle and living creatures of their kind to multiply, for the trees and plant life to multiply; all that had seed in it to bring forth in abundance (Genesis 1:9–12).

In Genesis 2:1–3, we first find the rest, or this temporary stop of work for the purpose of what God commanded: for the plant life to grow, for the flowers for produce, for trees to grow to maturity, for all kinds of fish to multiply, for populations of all kinds of animal life to grow, and for all to spread out. It was also for man and woman to be fruitful and populate the world. They were to have dominion and rule over all. They had their part in the procreation in the world. This is what God commanded them to do. Then he blessed them to do it. That is, God enabled all to do as he commanded them to. This was their purpose in Genesis, chapter 1.

Genesis, chapter 2, verse 3, tells us that God rested from all he made and created. Trust me, however, God was not tired. There was no weariness in him. Isaiah 40:28 states, *Hast thou not known? hast thou not heard, that the everlasting God, the Lord, the Creator of the ends of the earth, fainteth not, neither is he weary?* There is no weariness in him so this verse is not speaking of God being tired, but it speaks of a temporary stop, and that stop was for the multiplying and maturity of all God had called into being.

Genesis 2:4 states that *these are the generations of the heavens and the earth, when they were created.* Genesis 2:5 explains that he (God) created them before they grew, so God called forth all these, including animals and man, as well as woman. They were two by two, already fully matured, ready to do as he commanded; i.e., to be fruitful and to multiply.

Now a generation is at least 40 to 70 years. Genesis 2:3, when God put a temporary stop to his work, meant that he must have stopped or rested for at least 40 to 70 years, allowing his command of multiplying to be established in the earth. Today, we have many, many more trees, plants, flowers, birds, ocean life, cattle, and many other beasts,

The Genesis Brief: The Sin Factor

some known and some unknown to man to this day. Also, we have many, many more people, for God created man and woman in Genesis 1:26. *And God said, Let us make man in our image, after our likeness.* Verse 27 continues, *So God created man in his own image, in the image of God he created him; both male and female created he them.* Verse 28 says, *And God blessed them [enabled them to do their purpose, as well as God's purpose, and God said unto them, Be fruitful and multiply, and replenish the earth, and subdue it: and have dominion . . .*

Now 40 to 70 years have passed by, the earth has brought forth according to his command, and mankind has also brought forth. The man and woman that God has blessed to bring forth have done just what God told them to do. They had children. I suspect that they had twins, triplets, multiple children at a time. The children grew up to maturity, had sexual intercourse with each other, and it was all perfectly normal and natural, for this is what God commanded them to do: to be fruitful and to multiply.

There was no sin factor in these people, for God had commanded them not to do anything other than what they were doing, and that was to multiply. Because there was no sin factor, there was no death, so these people whom I will now introduce as "seed-purposed people" did not get old and die, but they only grew to a state of maturity. What that age is, I don't know. I can only assume it was 33, since this is when Christ finished his passion here on earth. So the seed-purposed people didn't die, nor did the plant life. The trees and plant life were put there by God in their mature state but did not grow up from the earth as of yet. They only brought forth and yielded fruit after its kind. The seed at this point didn't die. It only reproduced the fruit. (Genesis 1:11–12).

So death, as we know it, did not exist. Why do I say this? Remember that there was no sin factor in this process of life with the seed-purposed people, so if there was no sin, then there was no death, because death is a by-product of sin. And if no sin, then no death (Genesis 2:16–17). God commands Adam not to take of the tree of the knowledge of good and evil, and it was only after sin came into the world, through the disobedience of Adam, that death was a factor. Genesis 2:17 states, *For in the day that thou eatest thereof thou shalt surely die.*

God only commanded his seed-purposed people to multiply, replenish, subdue, and have dominion. The seed-purposed people were having children with one another by the commandment of the Lord. It was inbred in them to reproduce with their sister and brother, and this was very natural. It was very good, for God had commanded it so. Things went on this way for 40 to 70 years. The people on earth were without sin because these people had no covenant with God. Although they had a purpose with and for God, they had no covenant with God, much like Isaac and Ishmael. Genesis 17:19 tells us, *God said [to Abraham], Sarah thy wife shall bear thee a son indeed; and thou shalt call his name Isaac: and I will establish my covenant with him.* Verse 20 continues, *And as for Ishmael, I have heard thee: Behold, I have blessed him, and will make him fruitful, and will multiply him exceedingly.* Verse 21 states, *But my covenant will I establish with Isaac.*

Although Ishmael had purpose and God's blessing (enablement), he had no covenant with God. Isaac had the established covenant with God. This was the way it was with the Genesis 1:26 people. They had a God-given purpose and blessing (enablement), but not a covenant. This is why there was no danger from the devil regarding them. The devil was on planet Earth, but these people were no threat to the devil, for they were not in covenant with God. There was no righteous bloodline to come from these seed-purposed people alone. They were only in line with God's purpose for the population of people.

Genesis 2:5 begins the journey into the covenant man. After 40 to 70 years of seed-purposed people, God then decides to establish a covenant people, in order that his great love could be expressed on this earth . . . in order that love could be proven both to us and to him through us. Both would require a great sacrifice. Genesis, chapter 2, verse 5, now introduces this covenant mankind. Genesis 2:5 reads, *And every plant of the field before it was in the earth, and every herb of the field before it grew* . . . So plant life was reproducing itself from a live seed. Seed did not die before the covenant man. Seed only reproduced itself after it was fully mature, the same as the seed-purposed people did not die but kept on reproducing after their kind.

Let's go on. Genesis 2:5 says there had been no rain on earth, because there was not a man (mankind) to till the ground. Now, Genesis 1:26 tells us that God had already established not only a man, but a woman, and told them what he wanted out of them. He gave them a commandment to be fruitful, to multiply, to subdue, and to have dominion over all. God blesses them and enables them to do just that. This is not a contradiction. It is two different people for two different purposes in this world.

Genesis 2:7 begins to establish the differences of these two different groups of people. *And the Lord God formed [not created] man of the dust of the ground.* So this man Adam was formed from a substance, from something already created. That's why Genesis 2:1 is not a contradiction, for when God finishes his creations, this Adam man was formed from something God had already created . . . the earth itself (Genesis 2:7). This man from the finger of God was *formed, not spoken* into this earth as was first man and woman. First substance, then formed, now this earth man, with form, gets the highest gift of all: the very breath of God. God breathed the breath of the Holy Spirit into Adam, and Adam became a living soul. Adam became more godlike than any other creation God had ever created, including the seed-purposed man, because God gave Adam the man a part of himself that we must receive when we ask Christ to be our Savior, that is, the power of Holy Spirit who makes us capable of communing with God the Father on the highest level possible. And this is what Adam man had: the Holy Spirit, a life soul, a living soul, able to communicate and have a pure, intimate relationship with God in its highest form.

God's breath is God's Spirit. His Spirit is a part of who he is, his ability to love, his ability to give, and his ability to prove his love and not be intimidated by his creation. For one can only be intimidated by another, if the other holds more. And God has it all—all power and all love because love is who he is. And there is no greater power than love. In other words, we can't be intimidated by someone that has less than we, but one can only be intimidated by someone that has more. Therefore, God the Father cannot be intimidated by anything that he has created or made.

CHAPTER Three

The Covenant and the Man

I can only begin to imagine how brilliant Adam must have been. Adam's cognitive abilities were probably unmeasurable on our IQ charts. A man created into a perfect world, a world untainted by bad memories, untainted by sickness, deformities, life disappointments, divorce, worries of the future, constant unfulfilled desires, lack of anything. Adam knew no sadness, no lack, no loneliness, and no disappointments of any kind. It has been said that Adam looked upon the animal kingdom and desired a wife because of loneliness, but I disagree, because before the fall, there was no loneliness. Remember, now, because loneliness is a by-product of sin, and there was no sin at that time.

The Genesis Brief: The Sin Factor

Genesis 2:18 says that God is the one that said, *It is not good that the man [this Adam man] should be alone,* and goes on to say, that *I will make him an help meet for him.* Recall that in Genesis 1:26, this mankind God made simultaneously. That is, God, at the same time, made both the man and woman. Whereas with Adam man, or covenant man, God placed the ability of woman in him, or the seed of the woman was inside of Adam. It was only after God had established the relationship and demonstrated the relationship with Adam did God bring woman out of Adam, and no one really knows how long it was before he allowed Eve to be manifested out from Adam's rib. Therefore, I can say that Adam was not lonely, as some might suppose.

I also have been told that God was lonely, so he made man, but God did not make man out of loneliness, but out of desire, and desire is not loneliness. If anything, this desire was for more . . . more out of love, not out of loneliness. More of himself to be expressed so more people could experience this vast love that God is. And in order for God to express himself (love), this holy God had to come into covenant with a man, and this man God started with was the man Adam . . . the first Adam, the first covenant.

Adam was not the first man on earth, but the first *covenant* man on earth. A godlike man with such abilities, such talents, such cognitive brilliance, Adam must have been the smartest man that ever lived, capable of asking God such mind-boggling questions, such as, what ingredients do leaves contain? . . . And more than that. Adam surely had the ability to understand the matter, and never having gone to a higher university, never having to experiment to find out how and why, but just being able to cognitively understand once told to him by God. Adam, already equipped with a mind full of understanding, very capable of understanding the answers he asked God. Wow!! So many times I've ask God what a simple dream he has given me means, and then I find myself saying, "But, God, I don't understand." This too is a by-product of what sin has done through the ages of time. But this is not what Adam experienced before the Fall. Adam and God, through the holy breath of God, experienced the complete joy of relationship . . . In a pure, untainted, perfect world.

CHAPTER Four

Adam's Covenant Partner, the Help Meet

Genesis 2:7 tells us that God has formed a new man, a covenant man, by the name of Adam. God then takes this man Adam and places him in a garden that God himself has made. God has given Adam a prototype of the garden of God since Adam and God are in covenant with each other. God gives Adam a look-alike of his garden. Genesis 2:12 and Revelation 22:1-2 shows the river flowing out, with pure gold in the land, onyx stone, bdellium, which is a ground cover that is very fragrant. This, by the way, is also a similitude of what the sons of Keturah and Abraham received from their father Abraham (Genesis 25:6), and what the wise men took to the baby Jesus (Matthew 2:1, 11). Genesis 25:6 reads, *But unto his sons of* his concubines, which Abraham had, Abraham gave gifts, and sent them away from Isaac his son [son of the covenant], while he yet lived, eastward, unto the east country. Matthew 2:1 reads, *There came wise men from the east to Jerusalem.* Verse 11 reads, *They presented unto him gifts; gold, and frankincense and myrrh* (gold for deity, frankincense is a sweet-smelling fragrance, and myrrh is what they embalmed with in the Bible days).

God places Adam in this beautiful garden to enjoy it for his living pleasure. *Eden* means "pleasure," and I am sure Adam was doing just that . . . enjoying the pleasures of his garden. This is also where we find that God has placed two trees uncommon in earth, the tree of life, as well as the tree of the knowledge of good and evil, right there in the middle of the garden. God then commands Adam not to partake of one of the trees, the tree of the knowledge of good and evil (Genesis 2:8-9).

It is unknown how long Adam was in the garden without his wife before God said it is not good for the man to be alone (Genesis 2:18). Adam had been learning from

God of his beautiful creations. Adam had been getting acquainted with all the different species of animals. I am sure Adam was swimming in the beautiful waters of this clean, majestic river, enjoying the colorful fish, in a perfect climate, never too hot, never too cold, and never knowing the differences between the two extremes as it relates to being uncomfortable. Adam was dressing his God-given garden, and life was good. Good is all Adam was ever acquainted with. In fact, up until this time, God was always giving to Adam. The only time before the Fall that God took anything from Adam was when he took one of his ribs, and then God turns around and gives it back to Adam in the form of Eve, his help meet; his crown.

Adam had God, who is good, and although Adam was aware of others on the earth, I am sure that Adam knew he had nothing in common with these other people, and had no desire to get acquainted with them. His very awareness of them was enough. Adam knew there were other people on the planet, much like himself (Genesis 1:26). Genesis 2:18 states, God have said that *It is not good that the man should be alone.* God said this, not the Adam. *I will make [not create, like the seed-purposed people] him an help meet [a crown] for him.* A help meet for Adam, one that will crown the king of the garden and be the perfect crown for the perfect king in this perfect garden that the holy God has made just for the king.

Genesis 2:20 explains that Adam had given names to all the cattle, fowl, and beast of the field. But for Adam there was nothing or no one that was suitable for this king creation that God decided to covenant with. There was no one among the seed-purposed people that was suitable for the Adam man because these people were without a covenant with God. So Genesis 2:21 explains what happened. Now the seed-purposed people were capable of uniting with Adam to procreate, but this is all Adam would have had, because Adam was acquainted with God on a whole different level, a spirit-to-spirit level of communication with deep intimacy and understanding of God, his world, and God's purpose for this world, so had God permitted one of the others into Adam's world,

Adam would have still been alone in every other area of his life. Adam would have had a wife without any understanding of who he really was, because she would have been unequally yoked; human, yes, but unequal, trying to always find a way to change Adam to suit herself because of the lack of understanding of who and what God made him to be. This is much like what we do today. We choose someone out of selfishness, thoughtlessness, or without the knowledge of what marriage really means in the sight of God. So we error and find ourselves in a whirlwind of trouble.

Even as we see in Genesis 1:21-24, God has commanded the beasts of the field, the fowl of the sky, and the sea creatures to bring forth after their own kind. Even the animal kingdom is pure at this point.

Genesis 2:12 says that the gold of the land was good, meaning, the gold was pure. No carbon, no impurities were mixed into this gold. There were no impurities in the gold because the garden was perfect. It wasn't until sin entered before the animals began to crossbreed. God, being God, knowing all, of course, knew this. In Genesis 2:21, God puts Adam to sleep, and here is where God actually cuts covenant with Adam. It is said that the first blood that was shed was when God killed an animal to cover Adam and Eve for their sins (Genesis 3:21). But Genesis 2:21 is where blood is shed for the first time, when God put Adam to sleep. This, by the way, was the first time Adam ever slept.

Sleep is something the body does to replenish itself. Sleep is what the body needs when it is tired and worn down from the activities of the day, but the process of replenishing and tiredness is a by-product of something dying off, and before sin came, nothing was dying off, because there was no death.

Sleep is something a baby needs in order to grow. The baby's cells and body are growing and developing when asleep, but Adam came into the world fully mature, completely grown, with no death in him or on the earth itself. Adam was able to name all the nocturnal animals, all the night-blooming flowers, and swim in the ocean in the dark to name them. Wow!

God then takes from Adam a rib. Now, when God put Adam to sleep and opened him up, I am sure Adam was bleeding. Yes, Adam was a covenant man, but a man nonetheless, and if Adam got cut, or opened up, Adam would bleed and hurt. Adam would not bleed to death at that time, because death is a by-product of sin, and there was no sin at the time of the cutting of Adam, but this was God's way of the first types and shadows of things to come. God knew that without the shedding of blood there was no covenant or remission of sin (Hebrews 9:22).

We can begin to see where God, in types and shadows, is beginning to reveal his Son Christ Jesus in the very beginning. Adam, being a godlike man, a covenant man, now has his covenant partner come out of him. The same way Christ came out of God as his Son. In Adam's case, his wife, or friend, which means covenant partner, came out of Adam, because she was to be the same as Adam in relationship to who he was on the highest level. In Genesis 2:23, Adam declares, *This is now bone of my bones, and flesh of my flesh: she shall be called Woman, because she was taken out of Man* — or Adam man, or covenant man. There was sameness, yes, but also they were one in flesh and bone. And when a man is to be in covenant with the woman God gives to him, and they marry, they go back into each other with sexual intercourse, and then again become one, because of the shedding of blood, now through the hymen of the woman, the woman now sheds the blood, and they become one.

In Genesis 2:24, Adam declares, *Therefore shall a man leave his father and mother, and cleave unto his wife: and they shall be one flesh.* After God presents his Eve to Adam, as his wife, I am sure Adam had no need to begin to teach Eve anything. I believe Adam's wife came out of him and began picking up on the very conversations that Adam and God had while she was yet Adam's rib, because Hebrews 4:12 declares that God's Word is *quick, and powerful, and sharper than any twoedged sword, piercing even to the dividing asunder of the soul and spirit, and of the joints and marrow, and is a discerner of the thoughts and intents of the heart.* In Revelation 1:16, John, in the spirit on the Lord's Day, saw the Son of man who also spoke and out of his mouth went a twoedged sword.

I believe when Eve was still Adam's rib, that the words of God that were being spoken to Adam while God and Adam were communing together were heard and understood by Eve while she was yet Adam's bone marrow. I believe God's words cut to the very marrow of Adam, and when God cut covenant with Adam and brought Eve out, she was fully mature and fully aware of all the words God had ever spoken to Adam. I also believe that there was no need to then blow again his breath into Eve, because God had already blown his holy breath into Adam, *and man became a living soul* (Genesis 2:7). That same life-giving breath was also in Adam's wife, because what was in Adam merely came out of him, complete and fully equipped to crown her king.

Proverbs 12:4 says *A virtuous woman is a crown to her husband*. Now, Adam is a king with his crown, no longer alone, able to do as God commanded him to do . . . to be fruitful and to multiply after his kind. Genesis 2:25 goes on to say that they were both *naked . . . and were not ashamed.* Why no shame? Because . . . say it with me—shame is a by-product of sin, and there was no sin yet. And no one knows how long Adam and Eve lived in this blissful state before the Fall, before the fallen one decided to approach God's chosen ones, God's covenant seeds. How long did the fallen one watch before he came up with a plan to try to destroy what God had created? That we don't know. What we do know is that he did, and it was the same one he used before while Lucifer, was in Heaven. But God still had a plan . . . a plan that Lucifer wasn't aware of while he was still among the heavenly host. For God had a Lamb slain before the foundation of the earth, (Revelation 13:8). But Lucifer never saw him before he lost his first estate (Jude 1:6).

But what went wrong in the garden with Adam's covenant partner? Genesis 3:1 says *the serpent was more subtle than any beast of the field that the Lord God had made.* And, this, by the way, tells me that the devil uses different personalities for whatever he is trying to accomplish at the time. Let's go on . . . *And he said unto the woman, Yea, hath God said, Ye shall not eat of every tree of the garden?* My first thought of this was . . . if I saw a serpent speaking to me, I would have been the first one out of the garden, but then again, this is still before the Fall, and Adam and Eve knew no fear at this point, because . . . Fear is a by-product of sin.

Verse 2 states, *And the woman said unto the serpent, We may eat of the fruit of the trees of the garden.* Verse 3 continues, *But of the fruit of the tree which is in the midst of the garden, God hath said, Ye shall not eat of it, neither shall ye touch it, lest ye die.* It has been said that Eve was now adding to what God had declared, but I disagree with this. I believe God did say this, "neither shall ye touch it, lest ye die," because if Eve was just making this part up, then she would have been lying, and at this point, Eve couldn't lie, because there was no sin committed yet, and lying, again, is a by-product of sin. Therefore, if Eve wasn't lying, then where did she get this information from? Eve must have gotten this information when God was speaking to Adam before Eve was manifested, while Eve was still Adam's rib. Recall that God's Word is sharper than any twoedged sword. It pierced into Adam's bones, and into the very marrow of his bones, which Eve was a part of, so this is where Eve got this information from. She was not, and could not, lie before sin entered in. At this point, Eve was just in conversation with the serpent.

Verse 4 says, *And the serpent said unto the woman, Ye shall not surely die.* Here, we find the father of lies, the devil, the fallen one, lying to Eve with enticing words. The serpent was standing up on two legs, looking Eve right in the eyes, and lying to her. Remember, now, Adam or Eve had never heard a lie before. They were in a perfect environment with a righteous God communicating with each other daily. And truth is the only thing they had ever known up unto this point.

Verse 5 of Genesis 3 illustrates that the serpent continues to entice Eve with his lies, telling her, that is, telling them *both* — because Adam was right there listening, but Eve was the only one speaking back — (I know I left myself wide open for a discussion here, so I will move right along rather quickly!) that their eyes would be open, and they would be as gods. Eve was processing the devil's conversation much as we do. We hear something that sounds like it's good information, a good idea, but not a God-given idea, thinking . . . because it sounds good, maybe we will try it. And sometimes we end up in a world of trouble . . . as did Eve. I believe Eve was thinking, *Yes, yes, I want to be more like God. Yes, I want to know about this wonderful God that is always loving, always giving to us.* I believe Eve was thinking, *I want to be just like God, because God is so wonderful, and I want to be just like him* — as we all do — we that are born-again want to be just like God our Father — *we want to take on all the loving characteristics of God.* But just like Eve, we must make sure we get our information from the *right* source.

Eve, out of a pure heart, never having heard a lie before, and never having been tricked before, was deceived into believing the father of lies, the devil. Lucifer, while in heaven, did exactly what he told Eve to do: he took of the tree of the knowledge of good and evil. But he beguiled her into it, as he did the third of the angelic host, knowing it would cause a fall in their lives. So out of Eve's curiosity, not evilness, the same way Lucifer was not evil in the beginning, but merely curious while he was still in heaven, did he take. Eve, now fully persuaded, and her natural curiosity being piqued, especially being bedazzled by an animal speaking to her for the first time, probably thought this must be good, whatever this special animal is talking to me about.

We can see that all of Eve's five natural senses were involved in this process. She *saw* the tree was good; she *heard* the devil; she *smelled* the sweet fragrances of the tree, I am sure; she *touched* the tree; and finally, she *tasted* of the tree. Now, Eve was ready to see how she could be more like God. Eve took the forbidden fruit and gave it also to Adam, her husband, and he did eat thereof (Genesis 3:6). Eve was beguiled, deceived, but Adam wasn't. Adam knew he was about to die. First Timothy 2:14 reads, *And Adam was not deceived, but the woman being deceived was in the transgression.*

The Genesis Brief: The Sin Factor

Adam, at this point, didn't have the right to tell Eve not to take from the tree because Adam and Eve were on the same level. It wasn't until after the Fall that the man had rule over his wife. In fact, that was part of the consequences of her behavior: *he [her husband] shall rule over thee* (Genesis 3:16). Yet, Adam chose to listen to the voice of his bride Eve as she must have extended the forbidden fruit to her groom. Genesis 3:17 says it clearly, *Because thou hast hearkened unto the voice of thy wife, and hast eaten of the tree*. The scriptures are clear about why Eve took: she was deceived. But why did Adam, her husband, eat? And it seems Adam took and ate it without even a pause.

Again, we can begin to see order being set up for the future—the new covenant—the fulfillment found in Jesus Christ himself. John 3:16 boldly declares, *For God so loved the world, that he [proved it] gave his only begotten Son*. God the Father so loved mankind the he proved it by sending his most beloved, his only begotten Son, to save us—his bride—the church—as did Adam. Adam so loved Eve that he literally died for her, his bride, the same way Christ literally died for us, the church, his bride, for we are the bride of Christ. It was love proving itself . . . not that love had to prove itself, but this is what love does . . . It proves itself. Love is an action; love is a person moving on the behalf of another, and the greater the love . . . the greater the action. No greater love does a man have than he lay his life down for his friend (John 15:13).

The word *friend* means "covenant partner," and Eve was Adam's covenant partner. I believe that if Adam had asked God for another bride, and not accepted the forbidden fruit, and there was never ever any sin again, except the sin that Eve committed, then Eve would have been the only one in the world that ever sinned. And I believe God would have somehow still made a way for just Eve to be saved. God still would have sent his Son Jesus to save her. Matthew 18:12 explains that if a man has 100 sheep, and one of them is gone astray, would he not leave the 99, and go after the one which is gone? (See also Luke 15:4–7, Luke 15:10.)

Had Adam not made the choice to die for his bride, then maybe Adam's love for his bride would have been in question. But seeing that Eve was bone of his bone and flesh of his flesh, and love is all Adam knew, and all he could do. He chose to love Eve, even though she sinned, He (Adam) died, both for her, with her, and, yes, because of her. Ephesians 5:28 states it clearly, *So ought men to love their wives as their own bodies. He that loveth his wife loveth himself.* No, Adam knew just what he was doing, and he knew why. Adam so loved his bride that he proved it by laying down his life for her, just as Christ so loves his bride, the body of Christ, that he laid down his life for her. So love proved itself.

Not only that, Adam wasn't going back on his words when he spoke them, his own wedding vows, as recited in Genesis 2:23: *And Adam said, This is now bone of my bones, and flesh of my flesh: she shall be called Woman, because she was taken out of Man.* Verse 24 says, *Therefore shall a man leave his father and his mother, and shall cleave unto his wife; and they shall be one flesh.* The only Father and/or Mother that Adam ever had was God, so Adam honored his own marriage vows and left his heavenly Father and cleaved unto his wife.

Paul, in Ephesians 5:25, speaks to the husbands, saying, *Husbands, love your wives, even as Christ also loved the church, and gave himself for it.* Had Adam let his bride lie alone, she who being a part of him literally (his rib), Adam still would have died, and what would Adam do with the love he had for Eve? His love still would have been there for her. Adam would still have felt as if a part of him died, the same way, when we, the bride of Christ, sin today, we crucify him afresh (Hebrews 6:6).

After both Adam and Eve sinned, verse 7 says their eyes were opened. Their spiritual eyes had now dropped to a lower degree because of sin now in their lives. Now, everything had to be filtered through a sin-conscious soul. Everything they did had to be second-guessed, as do we today. *Is this you, God, or is this me* kind of a thing. Now they were aware that something was wrong with being naked, and shame enters into the picture, whereas before sin, they were naked and were *not* ashamed (Genesis 2:25). So sin brings awareness of evil and shame, and they, as some of us try to do, began to sew fig leaves together to cover themselves. But God, in his mercy, remembers his covenant with Adam when he put him to sleep and cut him and blood was flowing, so he killed an animal for the skin. Adam and Eve had already made themselves a covering with the fig leaves, but because God doesn't break his covenant, God kills an animal and covers them with the skins—as if to say, Adam and Eve are still my covenant people, because God doesn't break his covenant (Genesis 3:21).

Genesis 3:8 explains that God is now searching in the garden in the cool of the day, and since the garden was a perfect place, "cool" wasn't cold, because a cold temperature is not perfection, so in the cool of the day must have been an appointed time with Adam, when God and Adam decided to meet. God sent the breeze of his Spirit through the trees of the garden at a certain time, and Adam must have always responded . . . But this time

Adam is hiding, and God asks him, "Where are you?" Adam replies that he heard God's voice and hid himself, because he was afraid since he was naked. Naturally, Adam knew he was always naked. Neither he nor Eve ever had on any clothing before the Fall. But now this sin has made them not to listen to the voice of God, then it turns something beautiful (their bodies) into something that was perverted, something that needed to be hidden.

And the worst thing of all, Adam and Eve had taken the devil's fear. They were afraid. Fear and Satan are synonymous. Fear is a big part of the devil's character trait, and now, Adam is experiencing it. Wow, what an exchange! What a spiritual fall Adam and Eve took—not to mention the natural fall. Indeed, Adam and Eve's eyes were opened . . . opened to evil, something they never knew before the sin factor. Adam exchanged life for death, as did Christ exchange his life for death, but in doing so, because he is Life, and Life is greater than death, he received his Life again when he rose from the grave, and thus, he allows us who were trapped in sin by Adam to now be able to exchange our death for his Life. *You* can do that right *now*, just by asking Christ to exchange your sin nature for his Life-giving nature, and he will come into you and do just that. You will have a new life, and when you die, you will have life everlasting.

In Genesis 3:11, God asked Adam, Who told you that you were naked? Have you eaten of the tree, I commanded you not to eat? Verse 12 provides the answer to God's questions. Adam says, *The woman whom thou gavest to be with me, she gave me of the tree, and I did eat.* Genesis 3:13 continues the discussion, *And the Lord God said unto the woman, What is this that thou hast done? And the woman said, The serpent beguiled me, and I did eat.*

Now, I know it is commonly preached that Adam and Eve were playing the blame game at this point, but I disagree. What they both told God was correct. In fact, they were explaining the order of the events. Both Adam and Eve were with God the Father too long in the garden to think they could play some kind of a blame game with him and somehow get away with it. Adam wasn't trying to blame Eve. After all, Adam just gave up his life for Eve. Adam loved Eve, so why would he try to get her into trouble with God to save himself? No, Adam was saying the woman you gave to be with me, as opposed to the other women on the earth ... remember the seed-purposed people. There *were* other people on earth (Genesis 1:26). I believe Adam was just giving God a clear and precise answer. Eve did give Adam the fruit, and Adam did eat it.

Again, when God asked the woman her question, she also gave God a clear, precise answer, by saying that the "serpent beguiled me," and that is just what he did. First Timothy 2:14 reads, *And Adam was not deceived, but the woman being deceived was in the transgression.* Eve was telling God just what happened: the serpent did beguile her, and she did eat. This is exactly what happened; no one was blaming anyone. This is just how it went down.

Now when it came down to the serpent, God didn't bother to ask him what happened, because he is the father of lies. God just began to hand down his sentences. Adam and Eve didn't think that they could fool God. No, they were quite aware of the greatness of God's wholeness, and his holiness to think that they could trick him. Adam and Eve now felt where they were once whole, complete, and like God, they were now aware they were no longer whole. They were now incomplete. If anything, they were feeling less. They were afraid to try to trick God because they were now feeling incomplete and unholy as a result of their sin.

In Genesis 3:14, The Lord hands down the curse to the serpent. *And the Lord God said unto the serpent, Because thou hast done this, thou art cursed above all cattle, and above every beast of the field; upon thy belly shalt thou go, and dust shalt thou eat all the days of thy life.* God actually cursed this animal, the serpent. After all, the animal gave Satan permission to use him as a visual to speak to Eve. Animals don't speak ... then or ever, but they do have a voice box. If they didn't, the hissing sounds some make, or other sounds, would not be heard. So Satan used this animal, with his permission, to beguile God's covenant woman Eve. God cursed the serpent by stripping him of his ability to walk, craw, fly, skip, jump, run, hop, or any of the abilities all other animals have.

In Genesis 3:15, God now is speaking to the spirit the devil itself: *And I will put enmity between thee and the woman, and between thy seed and her seed;* [the seed of death, and the seed of life. Now he was speaking of Christ] *it shall bruise thy head, and thou shalt bruise his heel.* And thus, Satan is under our feet!! Praise God!! So now we must prove our love back to God by taking up our cross, denying ourselves, and following him.

What is taking up our cross, you ask? Well, it's denying ourselves . . . denying ourselves of the world, the flesh, the devil, and our earthly desires—fully following Christ. And consequently, we are the ones that are the better for it. We now must prove our love, knowing that we love him because he first loved us. We prove our love back to Christ because of sin. Eve gave in to the lie of Satan in the garden. Yes, Adam was standing there listening, but Adam had no rights over Eve at this point. Adam had no authority to rule over Eve or to tell her what to do, or not to do, before the Fall. It was only after the Fall that the roles changed and headship was needed. In fact, Adam ruling over Eve was a part of Eve's consequences of sin.

Adam had to only be responsible for himself and his own choices at this point. He chose to die for his bride as Christ chose to die for his bride, and I am so glad he did, but because of sin having entered in, we must now prove our love back to God. No matter how hard the journey, no matter how rough the road, I found out in my life if we keep going and keep following Christ, we can say with no regret: It cost everything, but it is worth it all! Following Christ is worth everything!!

Genesis 3:18 declares the *thorns and thistles shall it [the earth] bring forth to thee*. The earth is now preparing itself for the crown of thorns that is to be placed on the head of Christ in his passion. The earth had never before grown thorns and thistles. Weeds were not choking out other plants. No, nature was in perfect harmony, in perfect balance, in a perfect world . . . before the Fall.

Matthew 27:29 and John 19:2-5 tell of the account of the platted crown of thorns that was placed on Christ's head. Genesis 3:22 goes on to say that man has become *as one of us, to know good and evil*. Adam, Eve, the seed-purposed people, and the world at large never knew anything but love and good before the Fall. Now, all people, as well as the earth, are producing evil.

Genesis 3:22 goes on to say, *And now, lest he put forth his hand, and take also of the tree of life, and eat, and live for ever . . .* It is clear that Adam and Eve had never touched the tree of life before the Fall. Had they taken from the tree of life before the Fall, they would have had the wisdom not to be beguiled. Nor did they touch the tree of life after the Fall. Had they taken from the tree of life after the Fall, they would have lived in this fallen state forever . . . in a state of death . . . in a state of absence from God. In fact, they would have been the living dead.

Genesis 3:23 explains the end result: *Therefore the Lord God sent him forth from the garden of Eden, to till the ground from whence he was taken.* The very thing Adam was made from took care of him, always yielding her fruit, always producing life without any help from Adam. Now, however, Adam is taking care of the thing that was made to take care of him. Now, Adam must work the ground that once fed him without any work. Life as Adam once knew . . . a life of ease . . . was now over. This entire world is now changed because of the sin factor. Genesis 3:24 states, *So he [God] drove out the man; [out of the garden of Eden] and he placed at the east of the garden of Eden Cherubims, and a flaming sword which turned every way, to keep the way of the tree of life.* God made sure no one would touch the tree of life. I am sure that the Cherubim angels took the tree of life back up into heaven, where it still is, and will always stay, while, the tree of death (knowledge of good and evil) died out completely.

CHAPTER Five

The Children of the Covenant

Genesis 4:1 informs us, *And Adam knew Eve his wife; and she conceived, and bare Cain.* Verse 2 states, *And she again bare his brother Abel,* so now Adam and Eve of the covenant have two boys, twins. God is a God of relationships, so God allowed Adam and Eve to have twins so they wouldn't have to grow up alone. Cain and Abel grew up together, as twin brothers, so they could understand relationship and fellowship. Although there were other children on the planet, many, in fact, by now, they were different. Cain and Abel were still the children of God's covenant seed, God's covenant people: Adam and Eve.

Cain and Abel were told the same stories about God from Adam and Eve when they were growing up. Cain and Abel were taught the things of God, so they knew all things concerning their way of life, which was different from the seed-purposed people's way of life. Abel was a keeper of sheep (a shepherd), and Cain was a tiller of the ground. He cared for the dust of the earth in order to produce food for his life. While both were great occupations, both were very different, and both were very necessary occupations.

Abel was a shepherd, a type and shadow of Christ being the good shepherd. Abel dies at the hands of his brother, completely innocent, as Christ dies at the hands of his brethren, an innocent lamb slain not only by his brethren, but for his brethren, and like the first Adam, because of his brethren.

Both boys were born after the sin factor and were a product of the tree of the knowledge of good and evil. Abel was a part of the good, and Cain, a part of the evil, and both having the knowledge of right and wrong.

In Genesis 4:3, we see, *And in the process of time it came to pass, that Cain brought of the fruit of the ground an offering unto the Lord.* So Adam has taught his children that there must now be a sacrifice, a proving to God of their love for him, whereas before the Fall, God was the one always giving, always proving, by showing and giving to Adam and Eve. Now they are proving their love back to God by a sacrifice of what they now had to work for.

And in time, Cain brought of the fruit of the ground an offering unto the Lord. Verse 4 states, *And Abel, he also brought of the firstlings of his flock and of the fat thereof. And the Lord had respect unto Abel and to his offering.* Verse 5 continues, *But unto Cain and to his offering he had not respect.* God respected Abel, his character, as well as what he offered unto God. God respected Abel because of his heart. Abel had a pure heart, thus, he gave a pure offering. This also is a type and shadow of Jesus the good shepherd, whose innocent blood was shed. And it was a lamb that Abel offered, because a lamb was a clean animal. This too is a type and shadow of Christ. Christ being the first fruit unto God, the first son, a lamb, a clean sacrifice so the unclean could be redeemed.

Abel also offered to God according to his heart. We know a tree by the fruit it bears, or, where a man's heart is, there is his treasure also. God respected Abel because of his heart toward God. Who Abel was on the inside, was manifested through his sacrifice to God.

God says he had no respect for Cain, or his offering. It wasn't what they brought so much as it was the *motive* behind what was brought. God first says that he respects Abel. Abel's heart and motive were right toward God. Abel brought to God out of his love and respect for God, and it showed in his offering. On the other hand, God had no respect for Cain because Cain's heart and motives were evil, and that too showed in his offering. Cain was showing God through his offering his lack of character, his lack of respect, his lack of love, not only toward God (But how he must have felt about himself), Cain was already full of anger, selfishness, hate, jealousy, and fear. That's why Cain was able to kill his twin brother, the one that he grew up with and once played with. Cain was a product of the tree of the knowledge of good and evil. Cain was a product of sin, and it showed up in his conduct, and in his offering. Cain did not bring forth the first; instead, he brought to God any old thing, and at any old time he felt like it.

I'm sure this was not the first time the sacrifice was required of them, but Cain got weary in well doing . . . and did as he willed and not what was required of him. By now, the entire world was growing and changing. Sin was manifesting in all of God's creations. The seed-purposed people were changing; they began to start dying because of sickness, disease, malformations, deformities, mental deficiencies of all kinds. Old age began to set in. They began doing all sorts of ungodly things that they never thought of doing before the Fall.

Even the animal kingdom began to change, as well. Previously, lions and lambs were able to comingle. Now some became very violent, aggressive . . . evil. Deformities set in. Just as mankind began changing because of sin, so did the animal kingdom. Animals began to crossbreed, Before this, horses were pure horses, and jackasses, but then they began to mate and their offspring became mules, mixing the pure nature with the sin nature, or the intended purpose for a wrong or unintended purpose. All of mankind—the earth and the animal kingdom—was spinning out of control after the Fall.

Genesis 4:5 informs us that *Cain was very wroth, and his countenance fell.* Cain had much anger in him, and it showed up when God put his wrong on display (verse 7). God asks Cain (verse 6), "Why, are you angry, and why is it showing on your face? If you were to sacrifice to me correctly, I would have accepted it." This tells me that Cain *knew* what was required by God, the first fruits, and that he could either do what was right or what was wrong. He chose to do what was wrong because his nature was full of sin. Cain is so full of the sin nature that he goes into conversation with his brother Abel, just as the fallen one went into conversation with Eve in the garden. Cain must have persuaded Abel to go with him out into the open fields, away from mom and dad, or any safety, and verse 8 says, *Cain rose up against Abel his brother, and slew him.*

Now, this is the fourth time that blood has been mentioned in the Bible so far. The first time is when God cut Adam, when he put him to sleep. The second time is when God killed an animal to cover their nakedness. The third time is when Abel brings his sacrifice to God. And now, the fourth time, when Cain kills someone in the image and likeness of God. God is, indeed, a friend that sticks closer than a brother (Proverbs 18:24). And a friend that loves at all times (covenant partner); but *a brother is born for adversity* (Proverbs 17:17).

In Genesis 4:9, God is asking Cain, where is your brother Abel? Once more, Cain begins to produce the sin inside of him as he begins to lie to God and declares that he doesn't know. The anger inside of him almost sounds like a sassy, confused teenager as Cain then replies, *Am I my brother's keeper?* God then asks Cain (verse 10), What have you done? *The voice of thy brother's blood crieth unto me from the ground.* Abel's blood had a voice, because the life is in the blood. The righteous blood had been spilled by the hands of the unrighteous.

Leviticus 17:14 clearly states the importance of the blood. As with the shepherd Abel, the righteous seed of Adam, as with the Good Shepherd Jesus, his eternal life is in the blood. And we can only receive life through his blood.

In Genesis 4:11-12, God is pronouncing Cain's punishments to him. God says, *And now art thou cursed from the earth.* So now when he tills the ground, it would not yield her strength to Cain. And that *a fugitive and a vagabond shalt thou be in the earth.* In Verse 13, Cain complains to God, *My punishment is greater than I can bear.* In verse 14, he continues with his speech, *Thou hast driven me out this day from the face of the earth; and from thy face shall I be hid, and I shall be a fugitive and a vagabond in the earth; and it shall come to pass, that every one that findeth me shall slay me.* So, who is this "every one"? The "every one" Cain is speaking of are the first generation of people, the seed-purposed people that I referred in Genesis 1:26, mankind that populated the earth for at least 40 to 70 years before Adam, God's covenant man, was formed.

In Genesis.4:15 we are told, *And the Lord said unto him, Therefore whosoever slayeth Cain, vengeance shall be taken on him sevenfold.* "Whosoever" refers to the seed-purposed generation (Genesis 1:26). *And the Lord set a mark upon Cain, lest any finding him should kill him.* Once again, this is saying that there must have been other people on the earth at this time; otherwise, who are all these other people capable of killing Cain? Who are the people that both God and Cain are now speaking about unless there were others on earth before Adam?

After the punishment of Cain, Cain goes out from the presence of the Lord and dwells in the land of Nod (meaning, "Wandering") on the east of Eden (Genesis 4:16). Genesis 4:17 states, *And Cain knew his wife.* Cain's wife came from this same generation of people that God created in Genesis 1:26, a people that were on the earth for seed purposes, for the population of God's covenant people, Adam and Eve's sons, Cain and Abel. Now that

Abel is dead, Cain takes a wife from this other people. His wife bears a son, by the name of Enoch.

Following this generation of Cain on the earth, up to Genesis 4:23, there is another killing that has occurred in Cain's bloodline, where Lamech says to his two wives that he has now killed two men because they were trying to wound him (self-defense) and that if God shall avenge Cain sevenfold (who had no just cause to kill his brother Abel), then surely God would avenge him seventy and sevenfold, because his was done in self-defense.

The covenant of God is still going to be kept although the righteous seed was dead, but now through another righteous seed. According to Genesis 4:25, *And Adam knew his wife again; and she bare a son, and called his name Seth: For God, said she, hath appointed me another seed instead of Abel, whom Cain slew.* Verse 26 states, *And to Seth [another righteous seed or covenant seed], to him also there was born a son; and he called his name Enos: then began men to call upon the name of the Lord.* Righteousness was once again being birthed in the earth.

Genesis 5:1 tells us that this is the generation of Adam, whereas in Genesis 2:4, it says *These are the generations of the heavens and of the earth when they were created.* This is when first mankind was also created in Genesis 2. Genesis 5:1 is the book of the generation of Adam man, or God's covenant people: Adam-Eve-Cain-Abel-Seth-Enos. Genesis 5:2, *Male and female created he them.* Adam had Eve inside of him (his rib), and God called their name Adam, and Adam called her name Eve. But God called the first generation of people male and female: mankind. Genesis 5:3, *And Adam lived an hundred and thirty years, and begat a son in his own likeness, and after his image; and called his name Seth.* In verse 4, we see, *And the days of Adam after he had begotten Seth were eight hundred years: and he begat sons and daughters.*

Many believe that Adam and Eve had daughters before Cain and Abel, but that isn't scriptural. They believe this because of Cain's wife, without the understanding of Genesis 1:26 and Genesis 2:7. They are not the same people. This has always been overlooked, so some have "filled in the blanks" where there are no blanks to be filled in. It's quite clear that these are two sets of different kinds of people with two different reasons, and purposes, of being on the earth. One was seed, another covenant. The seed was to fulfill the covenant people of God, as in the case of Isaac and Ishmael. Same father, one with a covenant of God, and the other without a covenant. One with a purpose without covenant, and another with both purpose and covenant.

The first time Adam and Eve had daughters was only after God had reestablished his covenant seed in the person of Seth. Adam was eight hundred years old before he had ever had a daughter. Adam's purpose was then over at nine hundred and thirty years, so then he died. But not before the reestablished seed was born: Seth.

CHAPTER
Six

Sons of God

Genesis 6:2, Genesis 6:4, Job 1:6, Job 2:1, Job 38:7, John 1:12, Romans 8:14, Romans 8:19, Philippians 2:15, 1 John 3:1, 1 John 3:2: all these speak of a people of God, not of fallen angels. God doesn't call his holy angels his son, so why would God call fallen angels his sons (Hebrews 1:5)? *For unto which of the angels said he at any time, Thou art my Son, this day have I begotten thee? And again, I will be to him a Father, and he shall be to me a Son?*

In verse 7, God declares that he *maketh his angels spirits* (not a son). Sonship is to "come out of." Angels did not come out of God but were spoken into existence by God. In the book of Job 1:6, the sons of God presented themselves before God. We, the spirit of man, while yet in heaven, were sons of God, because God knew us before we were formed in our mothers' womb. We were the ones shouting for joy, in Job 38:7 just as Melchizedek was over the priesthood, sent from heaven by God (Genesis 14:18). Melchizedek, as special as he was, yet God did not call Melchizedek his son. Melchizedek was a type and shadow of Christ, a priest of the Most High God, *without father, without mother, without descent, having neither beginning of days, nor end of life; but made like unto the Son of God, abideth a priest continually* (Hebrews 7:3). So even this King of righteousness, King of Salem, King of peace, was not referred to as a son of God. Yet Melchizedek met Abraham while Abraham was only a Spirit still in Heaven Hebrews 7:10.

Fallen angels were never referred to as sons of God. These are only the covenant people that God refers to as sons of God. Genesis 5:6 all the way through verse 31 explains how Noah can be traced all the way back to Seth, according to who begat whom, starting with Seth. We can find Noah in this righteous bloodline, or covenant bloodline. Genesis 5:32 tells us that *Noah was five hundred years old: and Noah begat Shem, Ham, and Japheth.*

In Genesis 6:1, *And it came to pass, when men began to multiply on the face of the earth, and daughters were born unto them,* verse 2, *That the sons of God saw the daughters of men that they were fair; and they took them wives of all which they chose.* The sons of God were of Adam, Seth, and now Noah's generation, the covenant bloodline, and the daughters of men were of the seed generation of people. And they (i.e., the covenant generation) took them as wives of all which they chose. This is telling us that sin has made a huge impact on the morals of both the covenant people as well as the seed-purposed, or first generation of people. The sons of God refers to the covenant people, and the daughters of men refer to the noncovenant, or seed-purposed generation (not fallen angels as some suppose).

The sons of God, or the covenant seed, begin to see that the daughters of the first generation were also beautiful. Not only that, there were more of them at this point than there were of the covenant race, and although in the beginning they were for the purpose of seed, and they were multiplying for that purpose, to populate the earth. These first people are where Cain also got his wife from the seed generation, and this was right for him to do. But now, God's covenant people began to take wives of all they chose (the sons of God).

God's covenant people have become so sin based, so immoral . . . sin had polluted them and ruled over them, so that they began to choose wives just for the sheer pleasure of sex—uncontrolled, unrestrained, abused, misused . . . just for the fun of sex, just for sex itself to fulfill the lusts of the flesh. It lost its purpose for which it was intended in the beginning. And when something loses its intended purpose by their evil imaginations because of sin, it becomes a misuse of . . . which leads to abuse of . . . which leads to the breaking down of. The corruption of that leads to the end of Sin—when it is finished—brings death.

So when the sons of God (God's covenant people) begin to take as many of these women as they wanted, without any purpose in mind for them or for the children that were born to them, without any regards to where, how, or who were to care for these women or their children, when God saw his intended purpose was now being perverted, God said, in verse 3, *My spirit shall not always strive with man [meaning the covenant man, or the sons of God] for that he also is flesh.* Although God had a covenant with man through Adam, Seth, and now Noah, because of sin in the world, he determines to make changes. Man knows good and evil and has knowledge of sin. Sin is just what was going on with the sons of God (covenant people) at this point in Genesis 6:1-7.

So, God, now, begins to shorten the lifespan of mankind, to cut off the continual ungodly thought process. But still there is room for repentance. Verse 4 explains, *There were giants in the earth in those days.* What is a giant? An overgrowth; too much of something; more than average; greater in physical appearance than normal; in fact, abnormal. What brings about abnormalities is the sin factor, for before sin, there were no giants, or abnormal people. God made all perfect. But overgrowth, abnormalities, malformations, deformities, mental sicknesses are all a by-product of sin.

From the very beginning of this brief, I have tried to make this point clear. Well, the same is to be considered concerning the giants. These were malformed, overgrown people, from sin gone out of control, and God wanted the people to physically see that huge sin brings sometimes with it huge manifestations of the sin when continued, thereby producing huge, ungodly, unnatural people— some with six fingers and six toes on each hand and foot. It's all a by-product of their sin. That's why God raised up King David to kill off this unordered group of people, ones without a covenant, ones that were a by-product of sin. They were unordered of God. Giants (2 Samuel 21:15-22; 1 Chronicles 20:4-8). Their bones are being found even today.

Genesis 6:4 goes on to say that *There were giants in the earth in those days; and also after that.* These are they that King David and his men finally killed off. *The same became mighty men [strong, noticeable, capable of intimidating others, warriors because of their abilities] from men which were of old* (from first mankind, men of renown, men that made a name for themselves, through sinful acts, because of sin, when the covenant mankind and first seed-purposed people allowed sin to rule over them as it did with Cain. Then God allowed both people to produce and reproduce and become an enemy of his . . . Whereas before, God never had an enemy with a people, only with the serpent, the devil, and sin. But never with a people . . . until now).

Genesis 6:5 says, *And God saw that the wickedness of man* [sin was taking over and ruling over mankind] *was great in the earth, and that every imagination of the thoughts of his heart was evil continually.* What Cain allowed sin to do in him, in the beginning ruling over him, was now doing the same thing to both covenant seed as well as natural seed mankind, and has now produced such an overgrowth of sin and wickedness that people are turning out as a by-product of this now epidemic of sin. As Cain was a by-product of the evil of the tree of knowledge of good and evil, so has sin overruled both natural man and covenant mankind, the sons of God, and has produced a malformed race of people called giants.

In verse 6 we read, *And it repented the Lord that he had made man on the earth, and it grieved him at his heart.* Verse 7 continues, *And the Lord said, I will destroy man whom I have created from the face of the earth; both man, and beast.* The animal kingdom had lost its intended purpose as well. Animals were now being exploited by people (bestiality) and even the animals themselves begin to cross-breed within their own kingdom.

In Genesis 6:12, God says, *for all flesh had corrupted his way [purpose] upon the earth.* So God, makes a decision to destroy everything, with one exception. Genesis 6:8 states, *But Noah found grace in the eyes of the Lord.* God found favor in the man Noah, because of Noah's righteous or covenant bloodline. You can trace Noah's bloodline all the way back to Adam, and then Seth, the righteous bloodline, starting with Genesis 5:32 and backtracking who begat whom until you get to Genesis 5:3. Noah was God's next covenant man: #3. First, the father Adam, and Eve, being the mother of all covenant living; then the son Seth, the righteous living seed as is Christ; after which comes the rest, or comfort, Noah. And a type of the Holy Spirit bringing the power of a new beginning (Genesis 5:29). *And he called his name Noah, saying, This same shall comfort us.* Just as Holy Spirit is our comforter, he too was.

There are types and shadows woven in and out the entire old covenant, all leading up to our Savior Jesus the Christ. Wow! How great is our God!! Genesis 6:9 states, *These are the generations of Noah: Noah was a just man and perfect in his generations [Noah was just, but Noah was also perfect in his righteous or untainted, unmingled way, with the blood of this now abnormal people, the giants], and Noah walked with God.* Noah was given the righteous teachings from his father Adam, then Seth, and carried on to his father Lamech, and Noah not only listened to the words of righteousness but believed them, and thus, walked in the ways of God. But the earth was corrupt, and violence filled the earth. When God looked upon the earth, he saw the whole earth was corrupt; all flesh had corrupted his way upon the earth.

Because of sin, mankind, both, seed-purposed people, as well as sons of God, or the covenant people, had corrupted their purposes that God first ordained for them, to the point of no return, so God will now destroy man with earth (water). In the beginning, there was a watery earth in order to destroy this great sin and start over again with one covenant man as God did in the beginning, in this man called Noah (rest or temporary stop, in order to make again).

According to Genesis 6:13, *And God said unto Noah, The end of all flesh is come before me; for the earth is filled with violence through them; and, behold, I will destroy them with the earth.* Water purifies, water cleanses, water gives life, but water can also destroy life. The sea creatures in the waters of the oceans were always covered in a watery grave, always being washed and purified. The waters of the oceans were kept because as long as you are being washed by the water of the Word, sin can't rule over you. So the creatures of the oceans were untouched by sin, because they represent a constant source of the ever-flowing, living water of God. Everything that is in the earth shall die. The waters are not *in* the earth, but are *a part of* the earth.

In Genesis 6:14, God begins to tell Noah how to make the ark with wood, a type and shadow of the wooden cross, the ark meaning "Christ is our safety," and the ark of the covenant, for a covenant people. The measurements of it were as John the Revelator saw the angel measuring the city of God: a window above, as with the window of heaven. The door is placed on the side as he was pierced in his side. Then the ark was made with a first, second, and a third story, as with God being in the third heaven, the three in one: the Father, the Son, and the Holy Ghost.

Genesis 6:18 declares the Word of the Lord, *But with thee will I establish my covenant; and thou shalt come into the ark, thou, and thy sons, and thy wife, and thy sons' wives with thee.* Just like in Acts 16:31, where God tells us that you and your household will be saved if you believe in the Lord. If you have faith, and clearly Noah had faith, because Noah followed God's instructions to the very end, so he and his household were saved.

In Genesis 7:1, *And the Lord said unto Noah, Come thou and all thy house into the ark; for thee have I seen righteous before me [right standing and righteous bloodline] in this generation.* Verse 4 continues the story, *For yet seven days, and I will cause it to rain upon the earth forty days and forty nights.* Forty (40) is the number of testing, and then God would begin to destroy all. Noah was on earth 40 days and 40 nights before he and his household were actually shut in by God.

Genesis 7:11–13 tells us that Noah was 600 years old. Six (6), the number of seed mankind, and the number of people with him that were going to make that seed possible: three sons, three daughters-in-law = 6, but 8 altogether, totaling the number of new beginnings, because God keeps his covenant to a thousand generations. God is *still* honoring the blood covenant he had with Adam in the garden when he cut Adam open and Adam bled. And Seth did live, and Noah did believe. Now Adam's seed still lives on in Noah, in a purified world, with a new start.

Genesis 8:1: *And God remembered Noah.* God causes a wind to come, and the rains ceased and the fountains of the deep stopped. In verse 4, the ark rested, as did Noah (Noah, meaning rest) and his family, and all the animals were able to come out of the ark on the second month of day number 27, which would be according to the lunar calendar, Iyyar, that is in our calendar, late April, with 29 days in this month. So, Noah came out of the ark April 27th (spring) (Genesis 8:14-19).

In Genesis 8:20, the first thing Noah did after they were all out of the ark was he built an altar unto the Lord and gave a burnt offering, and the Lord smelled a sweet savour and promised never to destroy mankind again with a flood. As long as the earth remains, there would be seedtime and harvest, day and night, and winter, spring, summer, and fall (Genesis 8:21-22).

In Genesis 9:1-17, God begins to do the same thing he did in the beginning with mankind. He blesses them and gives them dominion over the earth. He enables them to replenish and multiply, and then he establishes a covenant with Noah. He promises Noah that he will never again cut off all flesh with a flood. God then puts the rainbow in the skies as a reminder to Noah of his promise whenever it rains.

Genesis 9:18 begins with the sons of Noah that came out of the ark. They were Shem, Ham, and Japheth. Ham is the father of Canaan. In reading this, it sounds as if Ham's wife had this child while on the ark; however, Canaan seems to be the fourth child of Ham (Genesis 10:6). Ham and his wife, more than likely, already had names for their children before they were to be born. For example, the firstborn son will be called Cush, the second born, if a son, will be called Mizraim, the third born called Put, and the fourth born, if a son, shall be called Canaan. As in the case of John the Baptist, the angel of the Lord said his name shall be called John. This was said to Zechariah, his father (Luke 1:13). Also, the Lord's name was foreordained to be called Jesus (Matthew 1:21). Abraham's son, Isaac, was named before his birth (Genesis 17:19), and Ishmael was named before birth as well (Genesis 16:11). Josiah was named long before his birth (1 Kings 13:2), as well as King Cyrus (Isaiah 45:4).

Genesis 9:20 states, *And Noah began to be an husbandman [farmer], and he planted a vineyard [grapes].* Time passed and Noah made wine, which was alcohol, so a fermentation process has gone on. Verse 21 states, *And he drank of the wine, and was drunken; and he was uncovered within his tent.* Alcohol makes people do strange things. Maybe Noah got drunk to deaden the pain he must have felt, seeing all his friends perish, those relationships he once had before the Flood. All his friends, and innocent children died. Perhaps Noah was reminiscing about the people that died, many he knew. This would surely be a reason, if one needed a reason, to deaden the pain of such a great loss. Perhaps getting drunk was in order.

Noah was drunk and uncovered, yet he *was* covered, because Noah was uncovered in his own covering; i.e., in his own tent. It's like being naked in your own house. Nothing wrong with that. But here we have Ham, his son, invading in on Noah's tent and privacy. Genesis 9:22

explains, *And Ham, the father of Canaan, saw the nakedness of his father, and told his two brethren without.* Noah and Mrs. Noah had their own tent; Ham and his wife had their own tent, as did the other brothers and their wives. For whatever reason, Ham went in his father's tent to see him. I don't know the reason. But something happened there so ungodly that Noah cursed his own grandson, that perhaps wasn't even born yet. The reason Noah didn't curse Ham is because God had already blessed Noah and his sons when God named Noah his covenant man (Genesis 9:1), and who God blesses, no man can curse.

Genesis 9:23 informs us that Shem and Japheth took a garment, placed it on both of their shoulders, walked in backward, and covered their father, so as not to bring shame to him. Genesis 9:24, *And Noah awoke from his wine, and knew what his younger son [Ham] had done unto him.* I believe Ham had homosexual desires. Ham was before the Flood, doing all manner of evil in the world, as the others in the world were doing. Remember, sin was rampant, running out of control. Wickedness and violence, evil thoughts continually abounded because of the sin factor which was out of control in the people, which is why God destroyed the world in the first place. Well, it seems that Ham had his part in that as well, and homosexual devils were in him. And perhaps in his wife as well. I only say that because these kinds of devils, homosexual and lesbian devils, are both the same kind of a sin against the flesh devils, and they seem to stay around each other.

But Genesis 9:24 states that Noah knew (was now aware) what Ham, his younger son, had done unto him, meaning . . . Ham had fondled, or touched, his father Noah, in an inappropriate way. Maybe Ham just laughed at his father was my first thought, but then, what is funny about one man seeing another man naked? They both are of the same sex, having the same body parts, so there is nothing funny about it.

When my mother was alive and she got sick, I took care of her. Many times I saw her naked, and I certainly saw nothing "funny" about that. We both had the same body parts. No, much more went on in Noah's tent; his son did an ungodly act, I believe. So vile was it that Noah cursed one of his own grandchildren (Genesis 9:24-25).

Genesis 10:15 starts to prove the curse of Ham's son Canaan, because Canaan was the first to begin to manifest the giant race again, after the flood. The blood, the tainted bloodline, came through Ham's wife. Ham's children's generation is the first time we see the giants emerging again after the flood. *And Canaan begat Sidon, his first born, and Heth, and the Jebusite, and the Amorite, and the Girgasite, and the Hivite, and the Arkite, and the Sinite, and the Arvadite, and the Zemarite, and the Hamathite: and afterward were the families of the Canaanites spread abroad* (verse 15-18). All these were giants, and enemies of God that King David killed off with his men (2 Samuel 21:15-22; 1 Chronicles 20:1-8). King David had completed his purpose in life.

And the same homosexual spirit that was with Ham, and the same lesbian spirit, the sin of the body, settled and developed in the land of Sodom and Gomorrah. This devil of homosexuality and lesbianism followed Ham and his wife all the way from before the Flood, to way after the

Flood, and developed and populated through their sons and daughters—an entire city filled with homosexuals and lesbians, and all sorts of evil and ungodly ways of living. It was the norm of the day there (Genesis 10:20).

Genesis 10:21-32 speaks of the sons and daughters of the righteous brothers of Noah, Shem and Japheth, and not any of their children or grandchildren were of the giant race. None were named in any of the (-ites) giant bloodline. Only the descendants of Ham and his son Canaan. Canaan was not only the race of the Canaanites, but the restart of all of the . . . giants, gods, unordered, ungodly, sin-bred, race of people. Genesis 13:13 reads, *But the men of Sodom were wicked and sinners before the Lord exceedingly.* But all of the giant generation after the Flood was restarted by Ham's son Canaan and his descendants (Genesis 15:19-21, Genesis 10:6-20).

Genesis 10:32 states, *These are the families of the sons of Noah, after their generations, in their nations: and by these were the nations divided in the earth after the flood.* Genesis 11:25 continues . . . *Terah an hundred and nineteen years, and begat sons and daughters.* Verse 26 informs us, *And Terah lived seventy years, and begat Abram, Nahor, and Haran.*

Genesis 11:27 states, *Now these are the generations of Terah: Terah begat Abram, Nahor, and Haran; and Haran begat Lot.* Terah, Abram's (Abraham) father's bloodline, can be traced all the way back to Shem, the pure or righteous bloodline of Noah (Genesis 11:10–26). Abraham took a wife, Sarai, a daughter of his father, from his father's concubine (a half sister). Genesis 20:12 reads, *And yet indeed she [Sarah] is my sister; she is the daughter of my father, but not the daughter of my mother; and she became my wife.*

Genesis 11:31 states, *And Terah took Abram his son, and Lot the son of Haran his son's son, and Sarai his daughter in law, his son Abram's wife; and they went forth with them from Ur of the Chaldees, to go into the land of Canaan; and they came unto Haran, and dwelt there*, as the Lord ordered him. Genesis 11 informs the readers that Abraham, by the hand of God, was extremely rich, along with his nephew Lot. They had so much cattle and land that it become too much for both of them to share the same land. Abraham gives Lot the choice as to what land to take for his wealthy lifestyle. Lot takes the best for himself, which is the land of Sodom, where the descendants of Ham have settled in and corrupted the land with all kinds of perversion and fleshly pleasures. So Lot picks Sodom and is most likely the big shot there because of his wealth (Genesis 13:10-13).

Abraham settled in another part of the land. This was the land of the descendants of Ham's son, Canaan, who called themselves the Canaanites, where Canaan himself first dwelt after the Flood. And Canaan's offspring also settled and corrupted the land of Sodom and Gomorrah (Genesis 10:19-20). God then tells Abram to get out of the land of Canaan. God begins to speak a blessing over Abram as he declares he will make his seed as the dust of the earth (as Adam was from the dust of the earth, a covenant people) so that if a man can number the dust of the earth, then his seed also shall be numbered.

Then Abram moved his tent and came and lived in the land of Mamre. The city is in Hebron, and there Abram built an altar unto the Lord. Abraham has had the sacrifice unto God passed down to him from generation to generation that first started with Adam, after the Fall. The sacrifice now required us, the covenant people, to prove our love back to God, with God being the first in our lives.

There was a war involving the kings of Sodom after a period of time had passed by, and a king of the Sodom lost the battle and kidnapped Lot and his family. Abraham and his men went up and recovered Lot and his family and the other people. They returned to Sodom where they lived again. Their goods were also recovered (Genesis 14:1-16).

Genesis 14:18 *And Melchizedek king of Salem [peace] brought forth bread and wine: [a type of communion] and he was the priest of the most high God.* (Melchizedek was the angel over the priesthood.) There are angels over all the angels; whatever the duties of each angel, whatever their job description; there are ranking angels over the division, the burning bush experience with Moses. There were cherubim that guarded the tree of life in the garden, after the Fall (Genesis 3:24). These were fire angels, but they had a higher ranking angel over them, the Angel over Fire (Hebrews 1:7). Lucifer was an angel over other angels while still in heaven, and even after the Fall he is still the highest ranking fallen angel over his fallen angels. He still has power. He still is a spirit, although fallen. He no longer has authority over God's born-again covenant people. God has given his people authority over all the works of the devil (Luke 10:19).

As with Melchizedek, the angel over the priesthood, sent from heaven by God to do God's will in the lives of this Abrahamic (covenant people) generation, angels are now being sent to earth to help God's people. However, before, in the garden, the angels were not doing God's bidding, as it refers to Eve. But in order that God could keep his covenant people from continually falling into sin, God began to send his heavenly angels to do his bidding, to help his people. *Are they not all ministering spirits, sent forth to minister for them who shall be heirs of salvation?* (Hebrews 1:14)

Melchizedek, the angel over the priesthood. Hebrews 7:15-17 reads *And it is far yet more evident: for that after the similitude of Melchizedek there ariseth another priest* (verse 16) *who is made, not after the law of carnal commandment, but after the power of an endless life* [Christ] (verse 17) *For he testifieth, Thou art a priest for ever after the order of Melchizedek.* Hebrews 7:1 reads, *For this Melchizedek, king of Salem [peace], priest of the most high God [ordered from heaven by God], who met Abraham returning from the slaughter of the kings, and blessed him.* Verse 2 continues, *To whom also Abraham gave a tenth part of all; first being by interpretation King of righteousness, and after that also King of Salem, which is, King of peace;* (verse 3) *Without father, without mother, without descent, having neither beginning of days, nor end of life; but made like unto the Son of God; abideth a priest continually.* Hebrews 7:10, *For he [Abraham] was yet in the loins of his father, when Melchizedek met him.*

No one knows when angels were created. We have no way of knowing how long ago angels were created, but we do know they were created in the third heaven where God abides. Angels are spirits. Spirits do not have the ability to procreate. They have no flesh and blood, no bones, no bodies as such we humans do. They are spirits, and have always been spirits. We also are spirits and were once in heaven. God made us humans but gave us a body and soul, with a free will, full freedom of choice. Melchizedek also has no ending, because he is an angel. Angels don't and can't die. They live forever in heaven or in hell. That's why God made hell. It was for the fallen angels, because they don't die.

We can begin to see how Melchizedek is an angelic spirit. We don't know of angels' beginning; they have no ending. They are without father or mother. Angels don't call God father or mother, nor does God call his angels his sons. Angels don't come out of God but were spoken into existence by God; created beings to serve his purpose.

God never sent his Son Jesus to redeem a fallen spirit. They have no flesh and blood. More can be spoken into existence, at the will of the Father, if needed. Melchizedek was able to meet Abraham even while he was in the loins of his father (not even in his father's seed) because Abraham's spirit was yet in heaven. As was the angel over the priesthood, Melchizedek was. That's where the angel Melchizedek met Abraham. While both were still spirits, before the earth was ever formed.

This brief was prepared to bring about a deeper look into the word of God, as it relates to the more profound things, in the word of God that we sometimes struggle for the answers to. My prayer is just that; for a deeper, longer look into the word of God. For deep calleth unto deep Psalms 42:7.

Overview of Brief Points...

#1 There were people on the earth before Adam. Their purpose was for seed. They were here for a generation 40 to 70 years before Adam (Genesis 1:26, Genesis 2:7). Adam was the first covenant man on earth (Genesis 2:7, Genesis 2:21).

#2 Lucifer came from heaven after having taken from the tree of knowledge of good and evil while this tree was in heaven, and he became evil incarnate (Genesis 2:9). Lucifer did the same thing to Eve as he did while he was in heaven (Genesis 3:1-6).

#3 We are the sons of God, not fallen angels. God has never called angels his sons, especially fallen ones. Angels don't have the ability to procreate. If Lucifer had the power to persuade one to have sex with him, even if this were possible — and it's not — it seems to me he would have started with Eve. After all, he was able to beguile her to take of the forbidden tree. The sons of God are always speaking of the covenant people, even in the book of Job. These were priests coming to offer to God, and Satan came (in spirit) among them to get permission from God to destroy them, his covenant people (priests). God knew they were unable to take on what the devil had in store for them, so he found the man for the job, that man being Job. We are the sons of God, not the fallen one, now or ever. (Genesis 6:2, Genesis 6:4; Job 1:6, Job 2:1, Job 38:7)

These sons of God were our spirits rejoicing while we were yet in heaven (John 1:12; Romans 8:14, Romans 8:19; Philippians 2:15; 1 John 3:1, 1 John 3:2).

#4 If fallen angels could make for themselves flesh and blood, give themselves all the necessary body parts, give themselves seed, make blood, hearts, lungs, and all the other components that go into making a person, they would be like the Most High God. No! All the devil needs to do is plant evil seed thoughts into a person's mind and he can make them do as he wills. He can at best inhabit a person's body, if allowed, as with the serpent in the garden, and there he can do his best work. In fact, if he did have his own body, he would be limited, because these bodies we have limit us to certain things. No, he does his best work in the *minds* of God's people.

#5 The giant generation of people came from the sin of the first people (seed people) and the sin of the sons of God (covenant people). Sin brings malformations such as six fingers and six toes. Sin brings deformities such as overgrowth like found in the giants (Genesis 6:1-6).

#6 Melchizedek was an angel over the priesthood, sent to earth for just the purpose to be the priest of the most high God (Hebrews 7:1-3, Hebrews 7:10-17).

The end of *The Genesis Brief: The Sin Factor* written by Sylvia Richardson, July 2014.

www.ingramcontent.com/pod-product-compliance
Lightning Source LLC
Chambersburg PA
CBHW032017040426
42448CB00006B/648